You Can Choose Christmas

Other Books by Clyde Reid

Celebrate the Temporary
The Return to Faith: Finding God in the Unconscious
21st Century Man Emerging
Help! I've Been Fired
The Empty Pulpit
Groups Alive—Church Alive
Let It Happen: Creative Worship for the Emerging Church
Dreams: Discovering Your Inner Teacher

You Can Choose Christmas

by
CLYDE REID

WORD BOOKS
PUBLISHER
WACO, TEXAS

A DIVISION OF
WORD, INCORPORATED

You Can Choose Christmas

Copyright © 1975 by Word, Incorporated

67898MP98765

All rights reserved.
No part of this book may be
reproduced in any form whatsoever,
except for brief quotations in reviews,
without the written permission
of the publisher.

Printed in the United States of America
ISBN 0-8499-2900-8
Library of Congress catalog card number: 75-17085

To

    Laurie
    Rick
    Robin
    and
    Kelly

my children, who love a good story and who have made my Christmases a time of joy.

ACKNOWLEDGMENTS

I am grateful that artist Patricia Collins, who illustrated an earlier book of mine, *Celebrate the Temporary*, was willing to take on this project as well. Her sensitive illustrations have helped me say what I want to say.

Friends, too numerous to mention, have listened patiently and reacted with helpful comments as I shared some of my Christmas-theory thoughts and stories with them.

I especially want to thank the many people who have written and phoned me asking how they could get this book reprinted. I think of Keith Skiles, Dr. Jim Anthis and many others. For them all, I am deeply grateful.

CONTENTS

There is a depth
        a reality
        a promise in Christmas
And this depth has nothing to do with the
holiday
        or families
        or receiving gifts.

It has to do with God's eternal promise
        that we can have a new life
            start over
            begin again
            be born anew.

If we want that.
That can happen.

PREPARATION—
ANTICIPATION

To really celebrate Christmas, not just endure it,
    we need to prepare.

Preparing for Christmas has little to do with
    shopping early
    or making lists
    or getting cards in the mail.
It is something you do for yourself.

We prepare for Christmas by starting now.
For instance . . .

What do you want out of Christmas this year?
(It may be only March, but never mind.)
What do you want *out of* Christmas?
Not what do you want *for* Christmas. But what
do you want *from* Christmas?
What would you like to have happen to
you? to others?

*   *   *

Do you want to bring joy to someone? To
whom?
Do you want to feel the deeper meaning of the
birth of Jesus?
Do you want a bigger, better office party?
Do you want to be reborn?
Do you want a lot of presents?
Do you want some time alone, time for you?

You may aim high or low, but your dream will
help decide what kind of Christmas it will
be.

You may choose to do nothing. You may wait and hope that someone else will make it a good Christmas for you.

And they may.

But what you do now can make a difference. You can choose to make it a good Christmas for someone else—and your own Christmas will be influenced.

Your anticipation *makes* things happen. Just like your anticipation of someone's birthday can cause that birthday to become something exciting. Your anticipation gathers energy around it and causes things to happen.

If you really anticipate Christmas, some beautiful things can happen.

So try anticipating Christmas—by starting now.

* * *

To anticipate Christmas is to forget the tinsel on the street lights in October.

To anticipate Christmas is to set aside a
     Thursday night
   to bake nut bread for some special person,
     surprising them and you.
   Or to macramé a hanger for a plant
   or to write a poem.
   *(It doesn't have to be great poetry. If it is
     written with love, that's all it needs. There is
     poetry in you whether you know it or not,
     and to release a few words of it can be a
     lifting experience.)

To anticipate Christmas is to decide now that
     miracles are possible, and that some *are going
     to happen!*

It is to stand out on the back porch, or on the
     roof, or out in the park for awhile on a
     clear, crisp night and think about Jesus
     being born—
          Hope and love coming into the world,
          A great man who cared,
          A mighty spirit.
          And celebrate that in your heart.

To Celebrate Christmas is

    To Dream
    To Hope
    To Remember
        and
To Prepare for Something Great
    To Happen

    To YOU.

YOU
CHOOSE
CHRISTMAS!

You can choose Christmas.
Just as you can choose no Christmas.
Let me explain.
You can choose for nothing to happen to you
    this Christmas.
You can choose to hold onto your pain and
    your anger and your sadness. And many
    people do.

Their sadness and pain and buried resentment
feel good. They're like old friends they don't
want to give up. At least they hurt and that
is a feeling. To have some feeling is better
than no feeling, many people reason. I have
known quite a few. And I've hung onto hurt
myself too often. If our energy is too
occupied holding onto old pain and old
grievances, there can be no Christmas for us.
No birth of hope. No deep joy.
But we choose. We make the choice to hold on
or to let go.
We choose our own happiness—or our own
lack of happiness.

*   *   *

If you choose Christmas, you may choose pain.
You may give a gift that is not received or is not
appreciated.
You risk some of yourself when you choose to
risk the experience of Christmas.

Most of the time, I have decided, the risk is
    worth taking.
Risk opens the possibility of rejection and of
    acceptance and appreciation.
Risk opens the possibility of more pain and of
    great joy.

If you are hurting too much already, you may
    not want to risk more hurt—this year.
But if you can risk some of yourself, you can
    CHOOSE CHRISTMAS!

*   *   *

You can open a door within you and say,

    I want Christmas.
    I want something to happen.
    I choose Christmas.
    I choose to look forward to Christmas

            and hope.

21

Christmas is a birth . . . the coming of new life.

What infant is waiting to be born in You?
A new skill?
An art?
A new life?

Have you always wanted to try oil painting but
were afraid to start?
Or sculpting?
Or mountain climbing?
Have you wanted to write a book? A poem?

What infant is waiting within? What new birth
trembling to be released? What new
potentiality wanting fulfillment?

Christmas is a birth . . . the coming of new life

in you.

THE
GREAT
SANTA MYTH

What is it we are *really* looking for at
Christmas? What is it we really want that
plunges so many into depression and despair
when it does not come? I offer this theory.

I suspect that deep down many of us are
carrying an unconscious Santa myth. We keep
on expecting Christmas to have its childhood
magic. Strange and wonderful things happening
around us, happening to us. Seeing a strange,
beneficent man in a red suit at the toy

department—a man who has the power to bestow anything he wishes. Then Christmas Day. Loads of packages appearing like magic during the night . . .

    Sleds Bikes Slippers
        Cowboy/Cowgirl Suits Candy
    New Pajamas Toys Games Trains
    . . . and all that.

Maybe Christmas was like that for us when we were little and still believed in Santa. And, unconsciously, we want it to be like that again.

Or maybe it never was . . . and we keep wishing it could be. That magical, childhood Christmas that will never be—not now.

So we go on grieving for it, wanting it, cursing fate when it does not come again. Feeling let down. Sad. Depressed. Disappointed.

Isn't it possible that we carry this childhood Santa myth with us year after year? Isn't it possible that the myth takes an adult form in our unconscious and goes on haunting us? Let me state the myth another way:

"This year at Christmas, the miracle, the longed-for miraculous event will finally happen. I

25

will receive an outpouring of gifts that will prove once and for all that I am greatly loved and wanted and accepted.

"There will, especially, be one gift that will come from somewhere, which will be so great, so overwhelming, so fantastic, that I will never need to doubt again. It may not be from Santa; but from some mysterious, parental source will come this great reassurance—from God, mother or somewhere."

But then Christmas approaches. And slowly the clues assemble. The mail is all in and the few packages have arrived. Friends have come by with pumpkin bread and homemade elderberry jam. Some of the packages are already opened, and, while appreciated, they are not of the magnitude of the Great Gift. Once more, it is apparent that the great miracle has not happened. The huge package has not arrived. The Ultimate Gift is not there. The final proof has eluded us again.

So depression sets in. All the shopping and spending made no difference. The thoughtful gifts we sent didn't do the trick. The Great Gift from the Great Giver has not come. Maybe we are not lovable or acceptable after all. Santa has not appeared. The myth has failed.

So we limp through the holidays, going to too many parties, eating too much, filling up the time with too many events. We are tired and sad and curse the commercialism of the Christmas season.

I once saw a young man handed a small Christmas package. "Here's my Alfa Romeo," he said gleefully as he opened the gift. Could he have been unconsciously hoping for that Great Gift in the form of an expensive sports car—even in a tiny package?

This is Christmas for some. Take a black crayon and cross out the parts that don't belong to your story. Then add the details in the space below to fill in your version.

Now ask yourself: "Is Christmas hard for me because I am unconsciously waiting for the Great Santa myth to be fulfilled even while knowing it

won't? Am I waiting for that Great Gift to prove
to me that I'm okay—loved—wanted—accepted?"
One friend put it this way: "As a teenager, I
always felt let down when the gift-giving was
over. I was looking for that final okay—that gift
that would tell me I was loved."
Here is the myth alive in a teenager. Is it too
much to suggest that many adults carry that
myth in their subconscious? No wonder
Christmas is so difficult for them—another year
to fear because the myth will be shattered again.
My friend went on: "You know what I really
wanted? What would have proved to me that I
was okay? A puppy or a live animal! Or a car or
a TV or a stereo—something big."
The Great Gift. The elusive, the desired, the
ultimate. This is the five-year-old opening that
big box with the doll house or the eight-year-old
finding the bicycle—the great proof. The child
gets bigger, but the gifts get smaller. Are they
ever enough? My friend found her solution:
"I don't have that problem any more. I'm not
looking for that big okay. I gave it to myself. *I
know* I'm okay. So I don't have to get it in a
package any more."
The Great Gift is never enough even if it does

come. The gift is one we must give ourselves—
the gift of self-acceptance. No one else can
give it to us anyway. It is our birthright.

You can dump the Great Santa Myth too, and
free yourself for the creation of your own
Christmas. Put it in an old laundry bag, put
some rocks in with it, whirl it overhead and
throw it as far as you can. Then repeat this
incantation:

"O Great Myth, bearer of perpetual
disappointment, I now give you up to the
elements. I reject you. I deny you. I will not wait
for you any more. I need no gift to prove my
worth. So all gifts are a nice bonus. Begone,
Great Myth."

This incantation is best pronounced in a loud,
stentorian voice. Do not worry about the
neighbors. Do not apologize or be embarrassed.
You are exorcising a demon. Raise your arms to
the skies and call it out loud and clear.

And Merry Christmas.

CHOOSE CHRISTMAS

ALLOW YOURSELF TO FEEL

THE JOY
OF
CHRISTMAS

Joy is not something someone can give you. It
comes from deep within you . . . if you allow it.
  The joy of Christmas does not come from
    seeing tinsel on the lampposts at the
      shopping center
    getting an expensive Christmas card
    giving an expensive Christmas card
    opening packages.
It does not come from
  chocolate Santas

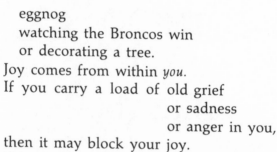

eggnog
watching the Broncos win
or decorating a tree.
Joy comes from within *you*.
If you carry a load of old grief
                    or sadness
                    or anger in you,
then it may block your joy.
If you do not allow yourself to feel
    anger,
    sadness or pain,
then you probably won't feel joy either.

You may have some "good" feelings, but real joy is deep. To feel joy is to be fully alive, to feel, to hurt, to celebrate. Real joy must be relaxed into.

I cannot advise you that you should allow your joy. You may not be ready for the full range of feelings—and that is the price for joy.

If you can experience joy, then you can feel the joy of Christmas. There is a special joy of

Christmas that somehow transcends all the tinsel.
It somehow brings together, fuses, uses,
enlightens
    the commercialism
    the pressure
    the meal
    candlelight
    loved ones
    the music
    and the message.

    If you can allow your other feelings, you can
feel that special joy. You must give it time,
quietness, reflection, meditation. Then it
begins—softly, gently, warmly—down in your
belly. It may never be overwhelming, huge, or
ecstatic. And again it may. But it can quietly
grow there and glow there, and if you allow it,
that joy can radiate a unique kind of energy
throughout your body.
    You can take a few moments now, listen for it,
and let it begin.

TO CELEBRATE
CHRISTMAS
IS TO
SHOUT
HURRAH!

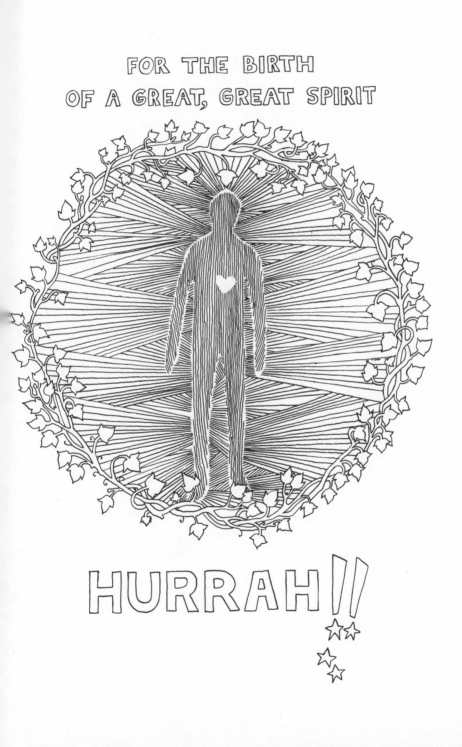

THE SADNESS OF CHRISTMAS

Christmas can be sad, too.
Christmas is sad for many people.
  They feel more lonely, more desperate, more
    lost.
  And Christmas never seems to measure up to
    their fantasies of what it should be like.

There is the fear of being alone and unwanted
    on the grand holiday of the year . . .
  the fear of feeling rejected

of feeling sorry for yourself
of feeling unloved
while all those others have someone to be with,
    someone who cares,
    someone to give them gifts.

No wonder the movies are full on Christmas
    full of the lonely
    full of runaways
    those trying to forget.
No wonder there are more who take their lives.

But being with people on Christmas doesn't
        bring that elusive happiness—necessarily.
Being in a big house with a lot of people doesn't
        help—necessarily. (Many people in those big
        houses are lonely, too.)
Feasting on holiday treats and opening packages
        doesn't make you happy—necessarily.
Sometimes it's just a lot of phoniness.
But knowing that doesn't really help when *you*
        feel alone and sad at Christmas.

*   *   *

So what should you do?

39

Allow your sadness. That's important.

Let it hurt. Of course it hurts. Everyone hurts
sometimes.

And hurting means you're alive. Pain is a sign of
health and aliveness.

Don't knock it. Allow it. Then look it in the eye.
Breathe deep and look the hurt,
the sadness, the pain
in the eye.

Why are you alone? Why are you sad? Why are
you hurting?

For some it is the myth of the Great Gift that
causes sadness.

For others, Christmas may bring memories that
make them uncomfortable. Christmas takes
us back
to the innocence of youth
to the days when our nuclear family was
together
to happier times
to the presence of loved ones now gone.

So we may be living in the past
and Christmas touches our unspent grieving.

It means we have unfinished business. When

40

part of us is hooked to the past, we are not
fully here.
We live with the ghost of Christmas Past, not
with Christmas Now.

So what can you do about it?
Have you invited someone to join *you?*
Have *you* reached out the way you wish someone
had for you?
What have you done to bring the aloneness on
yourself? Is it really necessary? Did you set
it up this way? Whom could you phone?
Who needs you?

But let yourself hurt. Let yourself cry if you need
to.
You can take some hurting.
To hurt is better than smothering the pain with
pills or pretense.
We don't need to be stuck with our sadness
forever. We can allow it its place—with the
help of a trusted friend—and let it out.
The great secret we then discover is that pain
and joy come together. When we turn off
our pain, we turn off feeling. Then we do

41

get depressed, because it takes energy to hold pain inside. Not to feel Christmas is sad in itself.

But if we allow the pain of our sadness, we may discover the deeper joy that is also in us.

To allow pain can bring joy! What a strange secret.

It was not a secret to Mary. She knew the pain of childbirth—which can hurt, no matter how thorough the preparation for natural childbirth. And in that pain, she also found the miraculous joy of bearing new life.

* * *

There is not a living person who has not known sadness and aloneness at times. The answer to it is within you, not in the decisions that others make for you.

Within you, deep within you, is the okayness that makes the sadness bearable. To find that okayness is like being born—and we are back to the joy of Christmas.

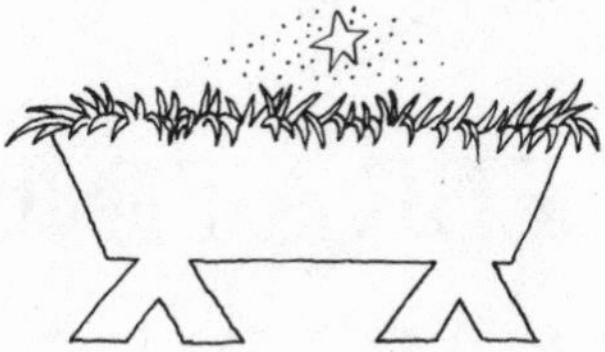

CELEBRATING
MEMORIES

Do you remember
   helping to pick out the Christmas tree?
      putting it in a holder and trying to get it to
      stand straight?
   hoping for snow for Christmas Eve?
   looking out the bedroom window in the
      middle of the night for a glimpse of a sleigh
      and reindeer?
Do you remember
   getting a neat shirt or blouse that didn't fit and
      couldn't be exchanged?

picking a chocolate from the gift box and
getting the hard one by mistake?
watching your chocolate Santa melt?
Do you remember
wanting to trade gifts with your brother?
running to show the neighbor kids your
cowboy suit—and seeing theirs?
getting a book when you wanted a football, or
a doll?
Do you remember
watching your first Thanksgiving parade with
that magic glimpse of Santa waving at all
the children before they took him into the
department store?
friends arriving at the door on Christmas Day
with packages in their arms?
being in the church pageant in a funny old
bathrobe and bedroom slippers with wings
fastened to your shoulders or carrying a
shepherd's crook?

Take a little time right now to recall some of the
fine memories you have from Christmases past.
There are some, you know. Give your memory
time to call them back and share them with
someone you love. They may bring some tears to

your eyes, but they will also warm your spirit. Allow your memories. They are part of your story. I will share this one of mine.

*   *   *

I remember waking up that cold, dark night in the old farmhouse. The only heat in my upstairs room was the faint amount that filtered up through the open register from the room below. I sat up and struggled into my unwilling slippers. Outside, the cold snow on the ground gave off an eerie light.

I knew it must be time. Santa surely must have come by now. The old eagerness and magic came over me as I slid into my familiar bathrobe and tiptoed toward the stairs. Every step creaked and complained as I went down, announcing my presence loudly. At the foot of the stairs, I eased the door open. There in the living room was the Christmas tree. My heart pounded. I was going to be first this year.

I moved toward the tree, eyes straining in the dim light—expectant, joyous. But there was nothing there. No boxes. No packages. It was exactly as it had been the night before. I blinked and rubbed my eyes as though that might change everything. Still no boxes appeared under the tree.

With the first traces of the early grey dawn in the sky, I knew Santa could not come now. It was too late.

What had happened?
What had gone wrong?

I only half-believed the Santa story anyway, but the gifts, at least, had always been there. Someone had seen to that. The myth had been maintained. If it was a game of Mom's and Dad's, they had always played it well—until now. There had always been packages at dawn to delight the early riser. And now the game had broken down.

I don't know how long I stood there. I know I had tears in my eyes. I felt disappointed and angry. Let down. Life was not the same. Something had gone out of it—forever. The presents were there by breakfast, but the myth was shattered and its broken pieces lay there among the piles of ribbons and tissue.

Childhood was gone. I was growing up.

GIVING

Giving is difficult for some of us. Some unconscious part of us holds back, forgets to follow through, or doesn't listen well to the person's real wants.

For a gift to have real meaning, the giving asks preparation:

What resisting is there in me to the giving of
this gift?
   Am I holding some anger I haven't shared
      honestly with this person?
   Am I afraid to make myself vulnerable to him
      or her by giving a really thoughtful gift?
What do I really feel for this person? What is it
      I am trying to say by the giving of this gift?
Do I want to say
   I love you
   I appreciate you
   I thank you
      or something else?
What does my friend enjoy?
   reading
   music
   drama
   psychology?
What can I give that would address his or her
      interests?

Do you remember
  making a gift for your mother at school?
  buying that first tie for your dad?
  the first time you had money to spend on
    Christmas gifts?
  the first Christmas present you bought for
    your girlfriend?
      or boyfriend?
        perfume? or a necklace? or shaving
        lotion?

  Giving has content: what shall I give?
  Giving also has style: the *way* we give the gift
may be more appreciated than *what* we give.
  I can remember friends stopping by with
cookies or Christmas bread and staying to help
eat it with hot coffee.
  I can remember a loved friend saying, "This
package is for you. It isn't a big gift, but it does
say that I appreciate you."

Somehow it makes a difference when the giver cares enough to hand you the gift, look you in the eye, grip your hand, or give you a hug, and say, "This is for you." It makes the gift more personal, more beautiful, more giving of *you*.

In the final analysis, *you* are the gift. If you do not honor *yourself*, then you will find it hard to honor your gift of *self*.

Honor you! There is only one you in this world and you have worth. You are precious. This is one of the most basic truths of the universe, even if you have difficulty hearing it.

That is why the birth of Jesus is so powerfully important. His coming to earth brought the reassurance of our worth as individual persons. He honored us. He found us worthy of great gifts. Should we not now honor ourselves as worthy? As having our worthy selves to give?

Forget what misled or unloved persons have tried to tell you. You are loved and lovable and worthy. And the gift of *you*, your love, is precious.

WHAT IS
A
GIFT?

A young woman stood waving at the airplane carrying her lover off to a distant place. Their Christmas visit was ended. As she waited, she noticed the woman next to her was crying. She asked and they began talking. It was a difficult time for the lady with tears and she shared the reason for her grief.

As the plane rolled away, the young woman proposed coffee and the two sat talking, sharing their common loss for a time.

It is easier to move away from those with pain. It is a gift to listen, to care, and to share that pain.

*   *   *

The true measure of a gift is in its cost. Not the money you spend, but the cost. What did it cost you? How much of you did you spend? How much of your love and caring is invested in the giving of that gift? The money matters not at all if the caring is there.

*   *   *

A true gift is a gift of love. True gifts don't come in packages. A mother takes her daughter aside and says, "I just want you to know that I feel you are a lovely person and I'm glad to be your mother."

A son sits down beside his father and says, "Dad, I want to tell you something." . . . "Yes." . . . Son waits while father lowers his newspaper. . . . "Dad, I've given you a lot of hassling in my day." . . .

"That's true."

55

"I just want you to know, Dad, that I also admire you and respect you. And I'm glad you hung in there with me while I was growing and testing limits. That's all."

Some of us are embarrassed to make statements of feeling like these. "I feel awkward when I get sentimental," they say. "My parents aren't the sentimental sort anyway."

Don't believe it! Underneath our protective layers, we are all sentimental. We are all feeling persons. If we use that for an excuse, we cheat our parents, our children, and ourselves of the loveliest gifts. It is worth the pain of a little embarrassment to let someone know you care and feel for them. It can open new depths in the relationship if you can pay the cost.

* * *

Sometimes we try too hard to put our gifts into packages. We have actually come to identify packages with gifts. If she gives me a gift, then she cares. If not, she doesn't care. This is a totally false identification of gifts and packages.

Try giving a non-package gift to each person you care about next Christmas.

A gift can be a three-line poem—written just for you.

A phone call.

A letter.

A remembering.

Some energy going from me to you.

*   *   *

I once saw a young woman pause beside an old lady in the back of a famous London church. The old lady was dozing. Her fingers stuck out through the holes in her ragged gloves. Without waking the old lady, the young woman quietly laid her gloves in the aged lap and moved on. What is a gift?

*   *   *

To tell someone "I love you" may be the loveliest gift of all. It can be said with strings on it that expect something in return. That is not a gift. When "I love you" is said freely with no expectations, no strings attached, no payoff, it is a lovely gift.

RECEIVING

Accepting a gift is difficult for many people. And we play little games with Christmas. I remember the one my dad used to play. He would always say to the family, "Now, I don't want you to get me a *thing!* We can't afford it, and there's nothing I need."

If we had taken him seriously and given him nothing, I know he would have been disappointed. When he would open his packages, he always said, "I told you not to do this." Perhaps he was protecting himself from the possibility that Christmas would come and there would be nothing for him. He could always tell himself, "I told them not to get me anything."

It is a gift to others to allow them to give you a gift. To receive a gift gracefully is a gift in itself.

Or we play another game when we receive a gift. We open the package and say: "Oh, you shouldn't have! I can't accept it. It's just too much. You shouldn't have spent your hard-earned money on me. You need it worse than I do. You must take it back." (And we're lying the whole time.)

This leaves the poor giver wondering if he has made some huge mistake. It takes away the beauty of the gift and leaves everyone with confused feelings. Sometimes this behavior is saying, "Let me do all the giving; it makes me feel important." Or we may be saying, "I'm really not worthy. If you give me gifts, unworthy as I am, I'll feel guilty because I know I do not deserve anything."

To receive a gift honestly and appreciatively is an art. It helps the giver feel good or feel rotten, depending upon our response to his gift.

There are many ways to respond to a gift:

"Oh, you shouldn't have done that." (I didn't give you that much.)
"That's very nice, but I'm afraid it's the wrong size." (Why did you get me *that?*)
Or we dismiss the gift with a bare response:
"Thanks—that's really nice. Did you see what Jim gave me?"

Or we can be simple, straight and honest:
"Thank you so much. That was really thoughtful of you, and I'm glad to have it."

TO EXPERIENCE CHRISTMAS
IS TO CELEBRATE

WITHIN US
THE BIRTH OF
PEACE
AND
JOY

THEY ARE THERE, YOU KNOW,
DEEP INSIDE,
WAITING FOR US

BIRTH

Christmas is a time of birthing, and a time to celebrate the miracle of birth.

Consider an ordinary birth—if birth can even be spoken of as ordinary. That tiny seeds, too small for the human eye, can carry life is a miracle. That those seeds can also carry the incredible complexity of the human body is beyond belief. Those seeds also carry the detailed differences that determine whether this child will be a male or a female, with all that implies.

The design of the human organs, the complexity of the brain, the beauty of the eye—all this and more is potential in one fertilized egg—microscopically small.

Is it any wonder we speak of birth as a miracle?

I have stood in the delivery room and watched with tears in my eyes and awe in my heart as my own child emerged into life. To witness this miracle is a deep privilege and fills me with reverence.

I cannot even begin to imagine how it feels to be the bearer of that life watching a child emerge from her own body. How much more of a miracle it must seem to the one who carries that life.

Christmas is a time to celebrate birth—the coming of new life into our world—the coming of new possibilities, new talents, but more important, a new *person.*

We also celebrate a special birth at Christmas. The birth of a special person whose life changed history.

We can celebrate Jesus whether we are Christians or not. By any standards, this man stands as one of the bright spots in human history.

We celebrate your birth, Jesus of Nazareth, and remember you as

> a prophet
> a visionary
> an exemplar of what you taught
> a bearer of light
> a teacher extraordinary
> one who cared for children
> one who healed
> one who saw
>   and understood
> one who gave himself.

Through your life, Jesus, love was increased in the world. Hope grew. Respect for persons expanded. God's nature was made manifest.

Because of you, Jesus, I can know that life has untold possibilities, immense heights, glorious potential. The low places are more tolerable, the depressions more bearable.

Because of you, Jesus, I know there is some grand intention, some Great Plan, some Source beyond us. Your whole life points to that plan and gives me

> hope
> joy
> and expectancy.

I'm glad you were born, Jesus. I celebrate the miracle of your birth.

THE COMING OF LIGHT

Christmas is a time of darkness—and of light.

By late December, the night is at its longest. If you live near the Arctic Circle, as people do in Fairbanks, Alaska, you have only a few hours of daylight. The darkness can be heavy, pervading. For some, it is depressing.

What better time for Christmas to come? The coming of the light. The return of the sun, with its warmth, its energy, its brightness.

Christ was himself light. He brought light into

our history and into our lives. He cared enough for us that his light has never gone out. It only gets brighter.

*   *   *

A young man once dreamed that he held an unlit candle in his hand. Nearby, Jesus stood with a glowing candelabra. The young man moved forward and Jesus lit his candle with his own. As the young man moved off into the darkness with his newly lit candle, eager to share his new light, his own breath blew out the flame.

The young man turned back to see Jesus still standing there, holding the light. He returned and hesitantly held out his candle a second time. The Christ did not blame or punish. He merely relit the young man's candle.

Again, he started. Again, he blew out his flame with the force of his own breath. Again, he looked back, expecting some reproach. No reproach came. Once more, the master relit his extinguished light. Once more, he started out.

This pattern was repeated, but the young man noticed one thing. Each time he had gone further before he lost his flame. With a lighter heart, he returned once more to the source and once more he started into the darkness.

*   *   *

We have a tendency to relate light with goodness, and dark with evil. Historically, darkness has been equated with danger, light with safety. But darkness is not evil. Light is not good. We need both. We need darkness and light to create shadows and nuances of shape and form. If we had all light, it would be boring. There would be no beauty, only monotony.

So we do not look forward to the coming of light as the vanquishing of evil. Rather, it is the sign of the continuation of variety in life. It is a reassurance that the universe still holds, that spring and summer will come once again. But would we want a world with only summer, no winter?

Celebrate the coming of the light.

Celebrate, too, the reality of darkness and the beautiful combinations of the two.

MY
FAVORITE
CHRISTMAS STORY

Christmas that year was pretty bleak. The Depression had hit us hard, and we didn't have much. There were jars of fruits and vegetables in the dirt cellar of the old farmhouse, but there was not much under the Christmas tree.

Aunt Elsie always sent a package for each of us from Nashville, and we were always excited when her box arrived in the mail. But there just wasn't much money for gifts that year, and Aunt

Elsie's packages looked lonely under the tree on Christmas Eve.

Mom was still fussing around in the kitchen, and Dad was reading the newspaper through for the second time, trying to squeeze some good news out of it, I suppose.

My older brother Baxter would come out the next day with his wife, Ardeane, and my sister Gene would come over from Bloomington with her husband, Don, and their first child. I must have been about seven or eight that winter.

A snowstorm had blown in around suppertime, and already there were about six inches of snow on the front porch. The wind was really howling, and we were glad to be inside. We all felt a little sad that there weren't many presents under the tree, but we pretended we didn't care. My brother Jim, being two years younger, had already put his p.j.'s on, and I was about to do the same when there was a stomping noise on the front porch, and then a pounding on the door.

We all looked at each other a little strangely as if to say, "Who could that be at ten o'clock on Christmas Eve in a snowstorm?" My dad peered out through the curtain a little nervously, then opened the door and said, "Can I help you?"

The man covered with snow on the front porch replied, "We're on our way to visit relatives for Christmas, and our car stalled in a snowdrift up the road a piece. Won't even turn over. I wonder if you might let us sleep in a corner somewhere until morning?"

I immediately thought of Bethlehem and wondered if my dad would let them sleep in the barn. He gulped a couple of times, but pretty quickly, he said, "Sure, bring 'em in! Can I get my coat and help?" Before you knew it, five people were trying to warm themselves over the one radiator in the floor of the living room—the man and his wife and three small kids.

By some miracle, hot cocoa appeared from the kitchen, followed by popcorn. Pretty soon, we were all sitting on the living room floor telling stories and singing some carols. It really felt good. The somber mood in the house had magically changed to one of joy.

After a while, people were yawning and looking tired. My mom got out all the extra blankets and took the pillows from Jim's and my bed. The family curled up in corners of the living room, and we all went off to bed.

I must have been first up in the morning. On

71

Christmas, I usually was. The snow and wind had stopped around midnight, and it was still outside. I wanted to peek at the strangers to see if any of them were up, but when I looked into the living room, they were gone! I checked the kitchen. Nope, nobody there. The bathroom door was open, so I knew they weren't huddled in there.

I looked out on the porch, but there were no footprints in the snow. Could they all have crammed into my folks' bedroom? I checked. Nobody there but Mom and Dad.

"Dad, wake up. The people are gone. Where'd they go?"

"Hmmm? What is it?"

"They're gone, kids and all. When did they leave?"

Curiosity triumphed over sleepiness and Dad rolled out of bed. "Whadda ya mean, they're gone? They can't be. And keep quiet; you'll wake everybody up." By this time, he was in his bathrobe and slippers and was peering into the living room. Nobody there. "I'll be darned. When did they go?"

"I don't know, Dad, but look on the porch. It stopped snowing during the night, and there aren't any footprints out there!" He looked, and sure enough, no footprints. We both put our coats on and hiked to the spot where the car had been stalled the night before. No car and no tracks. More mystery!

As we came back into the house, Mom had the welcomed smell of pancakes wafting through the place. And the coffee pot was bubbling.

We told her our story—no footprints and no car. She replied, "Isn't that strange? And did you see the packages under the tree?" I rushed in to look. I hadn't even thought about Christmas presents yet. Sure enough, there was a pile of gifts under the tree that had not been there the night before—and none of us had put them there! Of course, Jim was already seated in front of the pile looking through the gifts to pick the biggest one.

We never did figure out how they left or why, but we did enjoy those packages. It was a fine Christmas after all.

THE
DAYS AFTER

Christmas is gone now.

The tree is drying out and losing its needles.

The cards still trickle in, but today there was only one.

The glow is fading. Even the after-Christmas sales are fading.

The kids are heading back to school.

Winter lingers.

What difference does it all make? Was it worth the energy, the time, the expense?

What do we have to show for it? Some new

knickknacks, a new nightgown, an extra shirt.
Four more pounds around the middle. A bigger
bill to pay at the department store.
    If that's all we have, we don't have much.
    If that's all we have, it wasn't worth the hassle.
    I can tell you what I have:

        I have some nice memories.
        I remember some warm hugs and warm
            conversations.
        I see familiar faces that are now more real.
        I feel good about *me.* Some people I respect
            and care about have shared some love
            with me
                through cards
                through little personal notes
                by a word face to face
                a gift in the mail
                by being together
            and somehow that alone makes it
                worthwhile.

    But beyond the love and warmth of persons,
there is something more that remains:
        I have once again touched the mystery at the
            heart of the universe.

I have been reminded of the greatest gift of
   all
      God so loved the world (you and me)
         that he broke through into history
         in the form of a man
            who showed us that love of God for us.
And that makes all the difference.

   That's what Christmas means to me honestly—
this year. Next year it may mean less or
more—or something altogether different. What
does it mean for you?

                    *   *   *

   Light is returning to the sky. The days are
growing longer. Spring will come. Life begins
anew. The earth and ice will thaw. Growth starts
again.
   There is purpose. There is life. I, too, can grow
and begin anew, warmed by the life energy that
comes from beyond.